I0797841

**WIT AND WISDOM FROM THE WRITINGS OF JANE AUSTEN**

ILLUSTRATED BY MASHA LAURENCE

# CONTENTS

# Introduction

In a letter to her niece Fanny Knight, Jane Austen once wrote that 'wisdom is better than wit, and in the long run will certainly have the laugh on her side'. Undoubtedly, Jane herself had both wit and wisdom in abundance. Best known for her six novels, which have rarely been out of print since her death in 1817, Jane's romances have enthralled readers for more than two hundred years, while her witty dialogue and shrewd prose amused her contemporaries and modern readers alike.

Born in 1775 to George and Cassandra Austen, Jane began writing short stories and poems at the age of eleven; she preserved some of her earliest writings, known as her *Juvenilia*, including the epistolary *Love and Freindship* [sic] and the unfinished novel *Catharine, or the Bower*. Her first novel to be published was *Sense and Sensibility* in 1811, and three other books were published in her lifetime: *Pride and Prejudice, Mansfield Park* and *Emma*. Her two other finished novels, *Northanger Abbey* and *Persuasion*, were published posthumously in 1817, and she left behind a number of unpublished and unfinished works, including *Lady Susan, Sanditon* and *The Watsons*.

Most of what we know of Jane's personal life comes from her letters to friends and family. Her closest confidante was her sister Cassandra, who, after Jane's death, destroyed a great many of their letters; it has been suggested that she wanted to protect the rest of the family (and Jane's own legacy) from the frank observations and possibly scandalous revelations they may have contained. The letters that survive reveal a loving friendship between Jane and Cassandra, her thoughts on the notable people, plays, events and fashions of the day, and close relationships with other family members, in particular her niece, Fanny.

The chapters in this book are arranged by the themes that appear throughout Jane's works and her life: On Love, On Society, On Friendship, On Human Nature, On Reading, On Men and On Marriage. Quotes are taken from all her published works, some early writings and her private letters. Whether you are a lifelong Austen fan, a film-adaptation aficionado or even discovering Jane for the first time, this is a celebration of her wisest, funniest and most astute observations, many of which ring true even now, 250 years after Jane's birth.

ON
Love

'To be fond of dancing was a certain step towards falling in love.'

**PRIDE AND PREJUDICE**

'HARRIET WAS ONE OF *those*, WHO, HAVING ONCE BEGUN, WOULD BE *always* IN LOVE.'

**EMMA**

‘THE MORE I KNOW OF THE WORLD, THE MORE I AM *convinced* THAT I SHALL NEVER SEE A MAN WHOM I CAN REALLY *love*. I REQUIRE SO MUCH!’

MARIANNE DASHWOOD,
**SENSE AND SENSIBILITY**

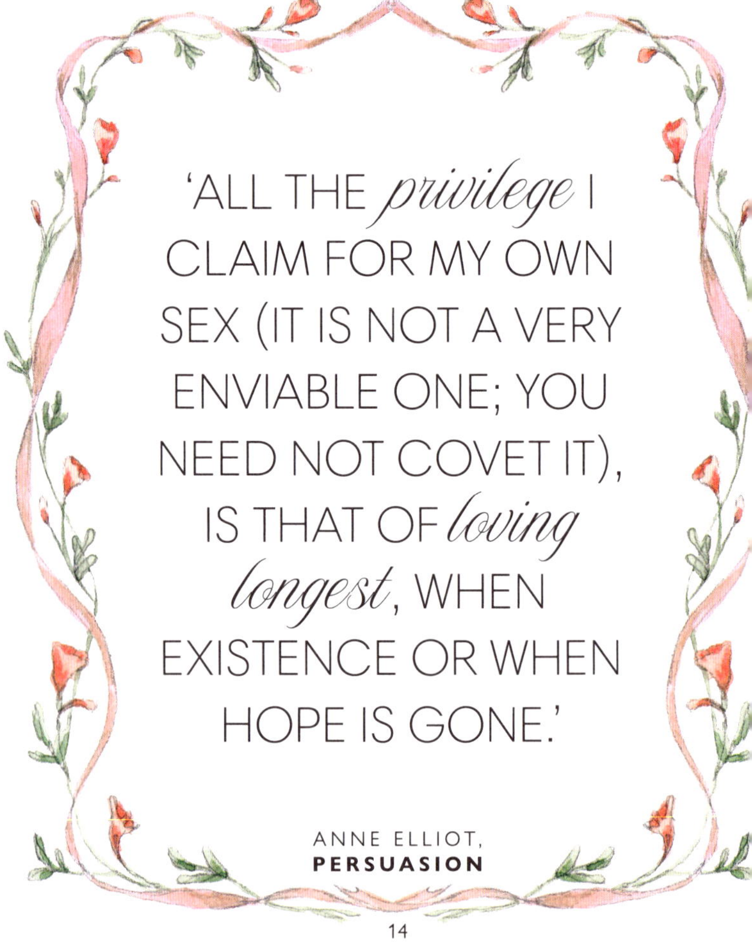

'ALL THE *privilege* I CLAIM FOR MY OWN SEX (IT IS NOT A VERY ENVIABLE ONE; YOU NEED NOT COVET IT), IS THAT OF *loving longest*, WHEN EXISTENCE OR WHEN HOPE IS GONE.'

ANNE ELLIOT,
**PERSUASION**

'Dare not say that man forgets sooner than woman, that his love has an earlier death. I have loved none but you. Unjust I may have been, weak and resentful I have been, but never inconstant.'

CAPTAIN WENTWORTH,
**PERSUASION**

‘Next to being married, a girl likes to be crossed a little in love now and then. It is something to think of, and it gives her a sort of distinction among her companions.’

MR BENNET,
**PRIDE AND PREJUDICE**

'THERE IS *safety* IN RESERVE, BUT NO ATTRACTION. ONE CANNOT *love* A RESERVED PERSON.'

FRANK CHURCHILL,
**EMMA**

*'You must allow me to tell you how ardently I admire and love you.'*

MR DARCY,
**PRIDE AND PREJUDICE**

*'If I loved you less, I might be able to talk about it more.'*

MR KNIGHTLEY,
**EMMA**

‘I SUPPOSE THERE MAY BE A HUNDRED DIFFERENT WAYS OF BEING IN *love*.’

EMMA WOODHOUSE,
**EMMA**

'To you I shall say, as I have often said before, do not be in a hurry, the right man will come at last.'

JANE AUSTEN, TO HER NIECE
FANNY KNIGHT,
**THE LETTERS OF JANE AUSTEN**

# ON *Society*

‘A single woman, with a very narrow income, must be a ridiculous, disagreeable old maid! The proper sport of boys and girls, but a single woman, of good fortune, is always respectable, and may be as sensible and pleasant as anybody else.’

EMMA WOODHOUSE,
**EMMA**

'I DO NOT KNOW WHETHER IT OUGHT TO BE SO, BUT CERTAINLY *silly* THINGS DO CEASE TO BE SILLY IF THEY ARE DONE BY *sensible* PEOPLE IN AN IMPUDENT WAY.'

EMMA WOODHOUSE,
**EMMA**

'By the by, as I must leave off being young, I find many *douceurs* [pleasures] in being a sort of chaperone, for I am put on the sofa near the fire, and can drink as much wine as I like.'

JANE AUSTEN, TO HER SISTER CASSANDRA,
**THE LETTERS OF JANE AUSTEN**

‘The older a person grows, Harriet, the more important it is that their manners should not be bad; the more glaring and disgusting any loudness, or coarseness, or awkwardness becomes. What is passable in youth is detestable in later age.’

EMMA WOODHOUSE,
**EMMA**

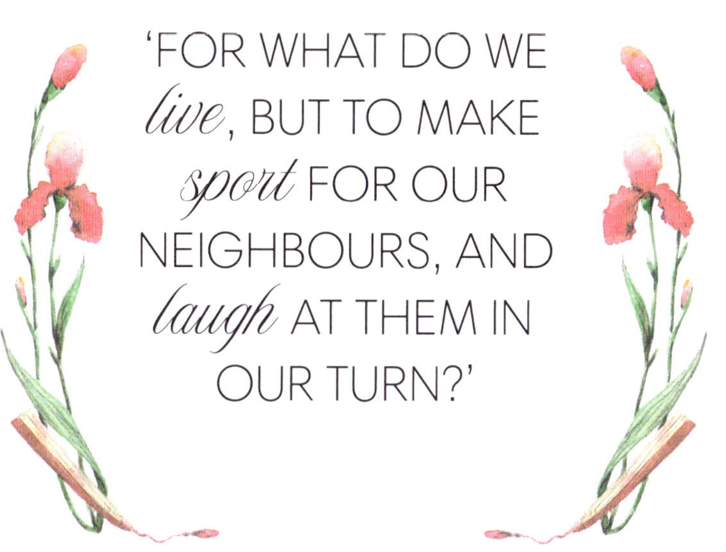

'FOR WHAT DO WE *live*, BUT TO MAKE *sport* FOR OUR NEIGHBOURS, AND *laugh* AT THEM IN OUR TURN?'

MR BENNET,
**PRIDE AND PREJUDICE**

'But you know married women have never much time for writing. My sisters may write to *me*. They will have nothing else to do.'

LYDIA BENNET,
**PRIDE AND PREJUDICE**

'BUT I HATE TO HEAR YOU TALKING SO LIKE A FINE *gentleman*, AND AS IF WOMEN WERE ALL FINE *ladies*, INSTEAD OF *rational creatures*. WE NONE OF US EXPECT TO BE IN SMOOTH WATER ALL OUR DAYS.'

SOPHIA CROFT,
**PERSUASION**

*'One half of the world cannot understand the pleasures of the other.'*

EMMA WOODHOUSE,
**EMMA**

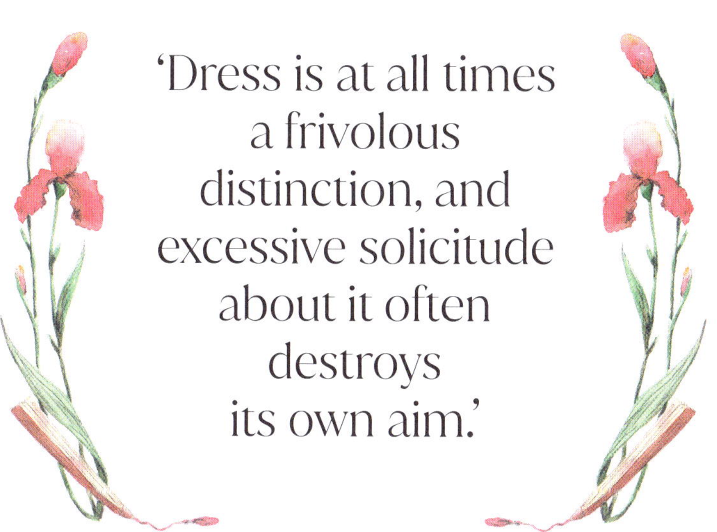

‘Dress is at all times
a frivolous
distinction, and
excessive solicitude
about it often
destroys
its own aim.’

NORTHANGER ABBEY

‘EVERY MAN IS *surrounded* BY A NEIGHBOURHOOD OF VOLUNTARY *spies*.’

HENRY TILNEY,
**NORTHANGER ABBEY**

‘The more I see of the world, the more am I dissatisfied with it; and every day confirms my belief of the inconsistency of all human characters, and of the little dependence that can be placed on the appearance of merit or sense.’

ELIZABETH BENNET,
**PRIDE AND PREJUDICE**

'HERE I AM ONCE MORE IN THIS SCENE OF *dissipation* AND *vice*, AND I BEGIN ALREADY TO FIND MY MORALS *corrupted*.'

JANE AUSTEN,
ON ARRIVING IN LONDON,
**THE LETTERS OF JANE AUSTEN**

# ON *Friendship*

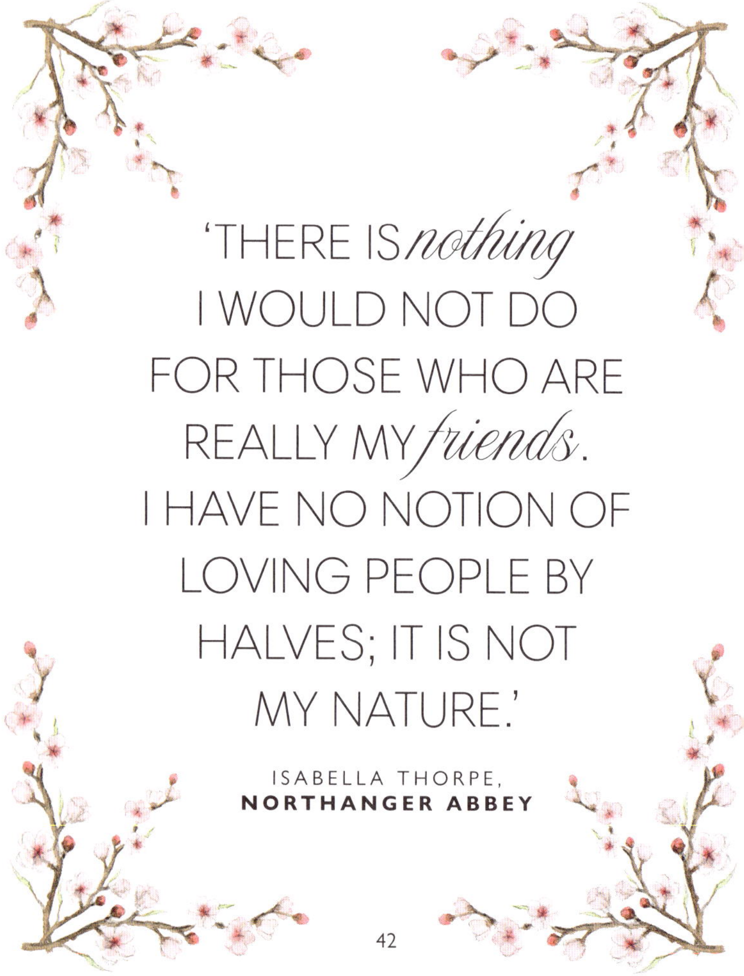

'THERE IS *nothing*
I WOULD NOT DO
FOR THOSE WHO ARE
REALLY MY *friends*.
I HAVE NO NOTION OF
LOVING PEOPLE BY
HALVES; IT IS NOT
MY NATURE.'

ISABELLA THORPE,
**NORTHANGER ABBEY**

'Business, you know, may bring money, but friendship hardly ever does.'

JOHN KNIGHTLEY,
**EMMA**

‘She had been a friend and companion such as few possessed: intelligent, well-informed, useful, gentle... one to whom she could speak every thought as it arose, and who had such an affection for her as could never find fault.’

**EMMA**

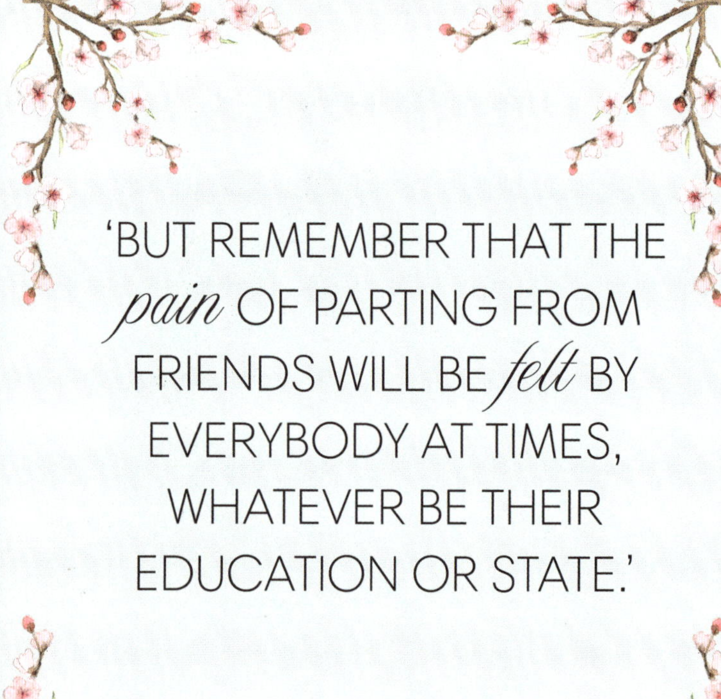

'BUT REMEMBER THAT THE *pain* OF PARTING FROM FRIENDS WILL BE *felt* BY EVERYBODY AT TIMES, WHATEVER BE THEIR EDUCATION OR STATE.'

MRS DASHWOOD,
**SENSE AND SENSIBILITY**

'She is probably by this time as tired of me, as I am of her; but as she is too polite and I am too civil to say so... our attachment [is] as firm and sincere as when it first commenced.'

MISS MARGARET LESLEY,
**LOVE AND FREINDSHIP [SIC]**

'Friendship is certainly the finest balm for the pangs of disappointed love'

NORTHANGER ABBEY

'You are so much used to live alone, that you do not know the value of a companion; and, perhaps no man can be a good judge of the comfort a woman feels in the society of one of her own sex.'

MRS WESTON,
**EMMA**

'THERE IS NOTHING SO BAD AS *parting* WITH ONE'S FRIENDS. ONE SEEMS SO *forlorn* WITHOUT THEM.'

MRS BENNET,
**PRIDE AND PREJUDICE**

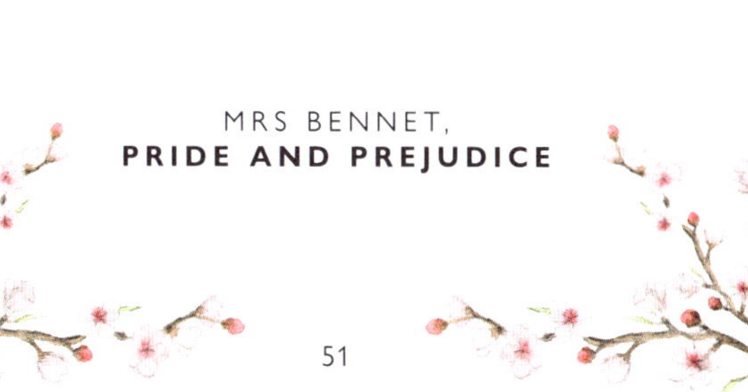

# ON *Human Nature*

'How quick come the reasons for approving what we like!'

PERSUASION

'NOBODY MINDS HAVING WHAT IS *too good* FOR THEM.'

**MANSFIELD PARK**

'It is very often nothing but our own vanity that deceives us. Women fancy admiration means more than it does.'

'And men take care that they should.'

JANE BENNET AND
ELIZABETH BENNET,
**PRIDE AND PREJUDICE**

*'Wickedness is always wickedness, but folly is not always folly.'*

EMMA WOODHOUSE,
**EMMA**

'I COULD EASILY FORGIVE *his* PRIDE, IF HE HAD NOT MORTIFIED *mine*.'

ELIZABETH BENNET,
**PRIDE AND PREJUDICE**

*'Those who tell their own story, you know, must be listened to with caution.'*

MR PARKER,
**SANDITON**

‘Seldom, very seldom, does complete truth belong to any human disclosure; seldom can it happen that something is not a little disguised, or a little mistaken.’

**EMMA**

'NOTHING IS MORE *deceitful* THAN THE APPEARANCE OF *humility*. IT IS OFTEN ONLY *carelessness* OF OPINION, AND SOMETIMES AN INDIRECT *boast*.'

MR DARCY,
**PRIDE AND PREJUDICE**

'SELFISHNESS MUST ALWAYS BE *forgiven*, YOU KNOW, BECAUSE THERE IS NO HOPE OF A *cure*.'

MISS CRAWFORD,
**MANSFIELD PARK**

PRIDE AND PREJUDICE

'NOTHING EVER *fatigues* ME BUT *doing* WHAT I DO NOT LIKE.'

MISS CRAWFORD,
**MANSFIELD PARK**

# ON *Reading*

‘The person, be it gentleman or lady, who has not pleasure in a good novel, must be intolerably stupid.’

HENRY TILNEY,
**NORTHANGER ABBEY**

'A *fondness* FOR READING... PROPERLY DIRECTED, MUST BE AN *education* IN ITSELF.'

**MANSFIELD PARK**

'I declare after all there is no enjoyment like reading! How much sooner one tires of anything than of a book! When I have a house of my own, I shall be miserable if I have not an excellent library.'

MISS BINGLEY,
**PRIDE AND PREJUDICE**

'BUT FOR MY OWN PART, IF A BOOK IS *well written*, I ALWAYS FIND IT *too short*.'

CATHARINE PERCIVAL,
**CATHARINE, OR THE BOWER**

'It is only a novel... or, in short, only some work in which the greatest powers of the mind are displayed, in which the most thorough knowledge of human nature, the happiest delineation of its varieties, the liveliest effusions of wit and humour, are conveyed to the world in the best-chosen language.'

NORTHANGER ABBEY

*'With a book he was regardless of time.'*

PRIDE AND PREJUDICE

'BOOKS – OH! NO.
I AM SURE WE NEVER
*read* THE SAME,
OR NOT WITH THE
SAME *feelings*.'

ELIZABETH BENNET TO
MR DARCY,
**PRIDE AND PREJUDICE**

‘I am no indiscriminate novel reader. The mere trash of the common circulating library I hold in the highest contempt.’

SIR EDWARD DENHAM,
**SANDITON**

ON
Men

'It would be mortifying to the feelings of many ladies, could they be made to understand how little the heart of man is affected by what is costly or new in their attire... Woman is fine for her own satisfaction alone.'

NORTHANGER ABBEY

'Men of sense, whatever you may choose to say, do not want silly wives.'

MR KNIGHTLEY,
**EMMA**

‘THERE CERTAINLY ARE NOT SO MANY MEN OF LARGE *fortune* IN THE WORLD AS THERE ARE PRETTY WOMEN TO *deserve* THEM.’

**MANSFIELD PARK**

'ONE CANNOT ALWAYS BE *laughing* AT A MAN WITHOUT NOW AND THEN STUMBLING ON SOMETHING *witty*.'

ELIZABETH BENNET,
**PRIDE AND PREJUDICE**

‘The ladies here probably exchanged looks which meant, “Men never know when things are dirty or not;” and the gentlemen perhaps thought each to himself, “Women will have their little nonsenses and needless cares.” ’

**EMMA**

‘My dear Alicia, of what a mistake were you guilty in marrying a man of his age! Just old enough to be formal, ungovernable, and to have the gout; too old to be agreeable, too young to die.’

LADY SUSAN VERNON
TO MRS JOHNSON,
**LADY SUSAN**

'IF THERE IS ANYTHING *disagreeable* GOING ON MEN ARE ALWAYS SURE TO GET *out* OF IT.'

MARY MUSGROVE,
**PERSUASION**

'WHEN A MAN HAS ONCE GOT HIS NAME IN A BANKING HOUSE HE ROLLS IN *money*; BUT THEY DO NOT KNOW WHAT TO DO WITH IT, KEEP VERY LITTLE *company*, AND NEVER GO TO LONDON BUT ON *business*.'

LADY SUSAN VERNON
TO MRS JOHNSON,
**LADY SUSAN**

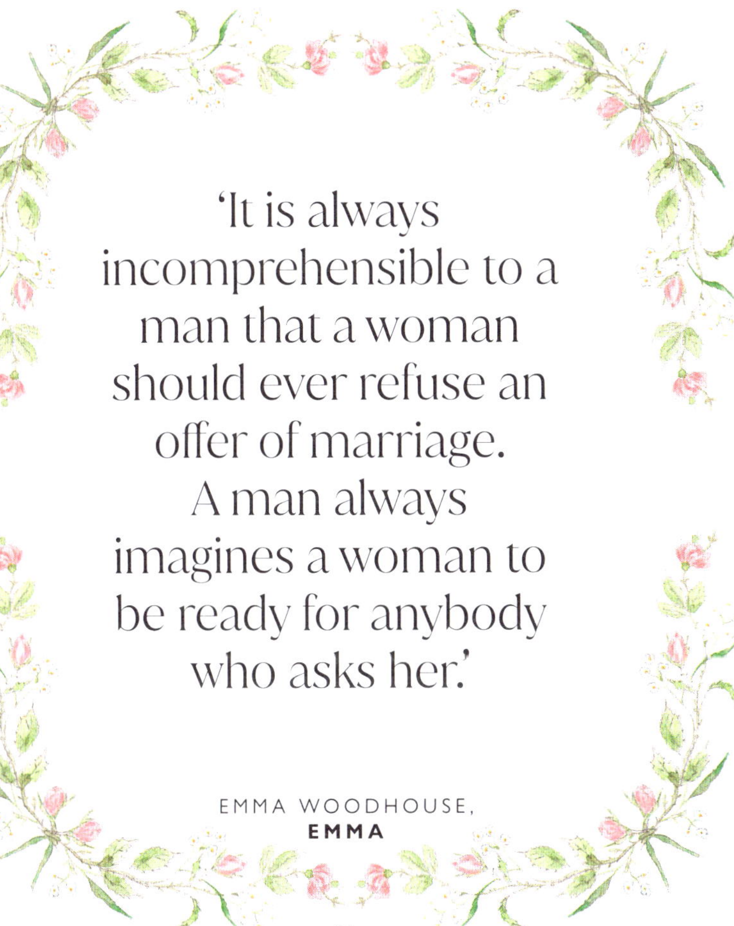

‘It is always incomprehensible to a man that a woman should ever refuse an offer of marriage. A man always imagines a woman to be ready for anybody who asks her.’

EMMA WOODHOUSE,
**EMMA**

*'What are young men to rocks and mountains?'*

ELIZABETH BENNET,
**PRIDE AND PREJUDICE**

‘I shall think with tenderness and delight on his beautiful and smiling countenance and interesting manner until a few years have turned him into an ungovernable, ungracious fellow.’

JANE AUSTEN, ON HER NEPHEW, THEN ABOUT THREE YEARS OLD,
**THE LETTERS OF JANE AUSTEN**

'A MAN WHO HAS *nothing* TO DO WITH HIS OWN TIME HAS NO *conscience* IN HIS *intrusion* ON THAT OF OTHERS.'

MARIANNE DASHWOOD,
**SENSE AND SENSIBILITY**

# ON *Marriage*

‘I have none of the usual inducements of women to marry. Were I to fall in love, indeed, it would be a different thing! but I never have been in love; it is not my way, or my nature; and I do not think I ever shall. And, without love, I am sure I should be a fool to change such a situation as mine.’

EMMA WOODHOUSE,
**EMMA**

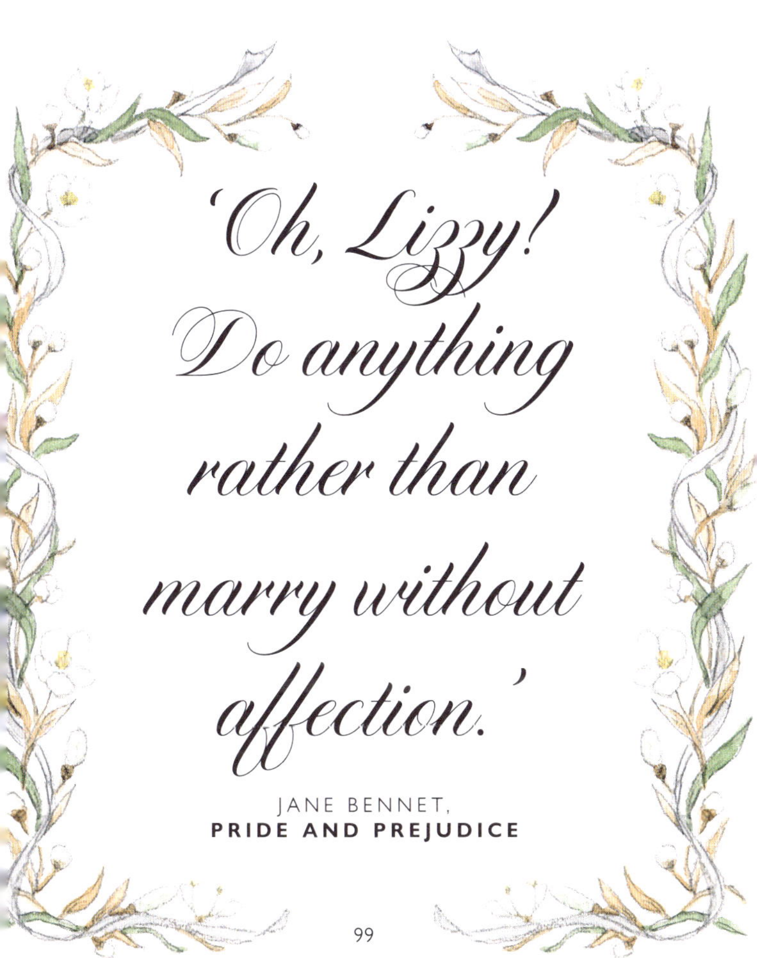

'Oh, Lizzy! Do anything rather than marry without affection.'

JANE BENNET,
**PRIDE AND PREJUDICE**

'A LADY'S *imagination* IS VERY RAPID; IT JUMPS FROM *admiration* TO LOVE, FROM LOVE TO *matrimony*, IN A MOMENT.'

MR DARCY,
**PRIDE AND PREJUDICE**

'If a woman doubts as to whether she should accept a man or not, she certainly ought to refuse him... It is not a state to be safely entered into with doubtful feelings, with half a heart.'

EMMA WOODHOUSE,
**EMMA**

‘It is only by seeing women in their own homes, among their own set, just as they always are, that you can form any just judgment. Short of that, it is all guess and luck – and will generally be ill-luck. How many a man has committed himself on a short acquaintance, and rued it all the rest of his life!’

FRANK CHURCHILL,
**EMMA**

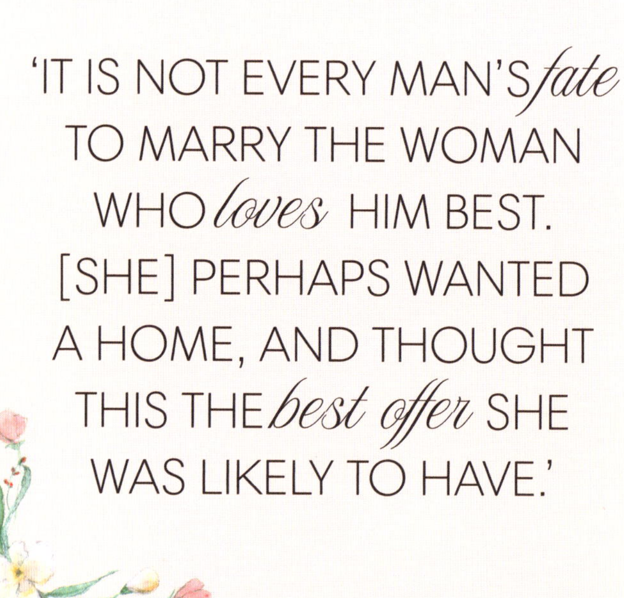

'IT IS NOT EVERY MAN'S *fate* TO MARRY THE WOMAN WHO *loves* HIM BEST. [SHE] PERHAPS WANTED A HOME, AND THOUGHT THIS THE *best offer* SHE WAS LIKELY TO HAVE.'

EMMA WOODHOUSE,
**EMMA**

'Husbands and wives generally understand when opposition will be [in] vain.'

PERSUASION

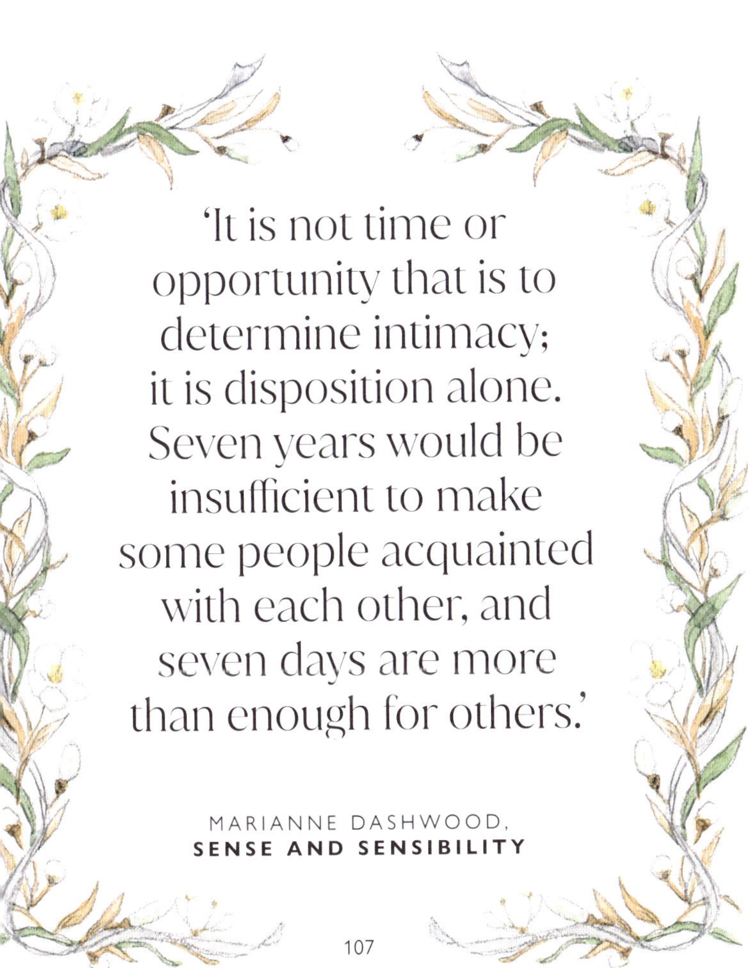

‘It is not time or
opportunity that is to
determine intimacy;
it is disposition alone.
Seven years would be
insufficient to make
some people acquainted
with each other, and
seven days are more
than enough for others.’

MARIANNE DASHWOOD,
**SENSE AND SENSIBILITY**

'*Single* WOMEN HAVE A DREADFUL PROPENSITY FOR BEING *poor*, WHICH IS ONE VERY STRONG *argument* IN FAVOUR OF *matrimony*.'

JANE AUSTEN, TO HER NIECE
FANNY KNIGHT,
**THE LETTERS OF JANE AUSTEN**

‘To be so bent on marriage – to pursue a man merely for the sake of situation, is a sort of thing that shocks me; I cannot understand it… I would rather be teacher at a school – and I can think of nothing worse –than marry a man I did not like.’

EMMA WATSON,
**THE WATSONS**

# SOURCES

## NOVELS

During her lifetime, Jane Austen never published under her own name; *Sense and Sensibility* was credited only as 'by A Lady'. *Pride and Prejudice* was attributed to 'the author of *Sense and Sensibility*', and so forth. Jane was only publicly identified as the author of her novels upon publication of *Northanger Abbey* and *Persuasion* after her death in 1817.

*Sense and Sensibility* (1811)
*Pride and Prejudice* (1813)
*Mansfield Park* (1814)
*Emma* (1816)
*Northanger Abbey* (1817)
*Persuasion* (1817)

## FRAGMENTS AND UNPUBLISHED WORKS

*Lady Susan* (dated 1794) – short epistolary novel, completed but never submitted for publication.

*The Watsons* (dated 1803) – unfinished novel, presumably abandoned.

*Sanditon* (dated 1817) – unfinished novel, never completed due to Jane's illness.

## JUVENILIA

Jane compiled her juvenile writings into three notebooks, entitled *Volume the First*, *Volume the Second* and *Volume the Third* and known collectively as the 'Juvenilia'.

*Love and Freindship* [sic] (dated 1790) – epistolary novella contained in *Volume the Second.*

*Catharine, or the Bower* (dated c. 1792) – unfinished novel contained in *Volume the Third.*

## THE LETTERS OF JANE AUSTEN

Jane's older sister Cassandra famously destroyed a great many of Jane's letters after her death. From those that did survive, an incomplete compilation (*Letters of Jane Austen: A Memoir*) was first published in 1884, edited by Edward Knatchbull-Hugessen, Jane's great-nephew and the son of her niece, Fanny Knight. Many other collections followed, most notably the R.W. Chapman edition (*Jane Austen's Letters to her Sister Cassandra and Others, 1796–1817*) published by Oxford University Press in 1932.

Quadrille, Penguin Random House UK, One Embassy Gardens, 8 Viaduct Gardens, London SW11 7BW

Quadrille Publishing Limited is part of the Penguin Random House group of companies whose addresses can be found at global.penguinrandomhouse.com

Published by Quadrille in 2025

www.penguin.co.uk

A CIP catalogue record for this book is available from the British Library

ISBN 978 1 83783 472 3
10 9 8 7 6 5 4 3 2 1

MANAGING DIRECTOR, PUBLISHING Sarah Lavelle
PUBLISHING DIRECTOR Kate Pollard
PROJECT EDITOR Ellie Spence
QUOTES COMPILED BY Judith Hannam
SENIOR DESIGNER Gemma Hayden
ILLUSTRATOR Masha Laurence
PRODUCTION DIRECTOR Stephen Lang
PRODUCTION CONTROLLER Sumayyah Waheed

Colour reproduction by p2d

Printed in China by RR Donnelley Asia Printing Solution Limited

The authorised representative in the EEA is Penguin Random House Ireland, Morrison Chambers, 32 Nassau Street, Dublin D02 YH68.

Penguin Random House is committed to a sustainable future for our business, our readers and our planet. This book is made from Forest Stewardship Council® certified paper.

## JUVENILIA

Jane compiled her juvenile writings into three notebooks, entitled *Volume the First*, *Volume the Second* and *Volume the Third* and known collectively as the 'Juvenilia'.

*Love and Freindship* [sic] (dated 1790) – epistolary novella contained in *Volume the Second*.

*Catharine, or the Bower* (dated c. 1792) – unfinished novel contained in *Volume the Third*.

## THE LETTERS OF JANE AUSTEN

Jane's older sister Cassandra famously destroyed a great many of Jane's letters after her death. From those that did survive, an incomplete compilation (*Letters of Jane Austen: A Memoir*) was first published in 1884, edited by Edward Knatchbull-Hugessen, Jane's great-nephew and the son of her niece, Fanny Knight. Many other collections followed, most notably the R.W. Chapman edition (*Jane Austen's Letters to her Sister Cassandra and Others, 1796–1817*) published by Oxford University Press in 1932.

Quadrille, Penguin Random House UK, One Embassy Gardens, 8 Viaduct Gardens, London SW11 7BW

Quadrille Publishing Limited is part of the Penguin Random House group of companies whose addresses can be found at global.penguinrandomhouse.com

Penguin Random House UK



Published by Quadrille in 2025

www.penguin.co.uk

A CIP catalogue record for this book is available from the British Library

ISBN 978 1 83783 472 3
10 9 8 7 6 5 4 3 2 1

**MANAGING DIRECTOR, PUBLISHING** Sarah Lavelle
**PUBLISHING DIRECTOR** Kate Pollard
**PROJECT EDITOR** Ellie Spence
**QUOTES COMPILED BY** Judith Hannam
**SENIOR DESIGNER** Gemma Hayden
**ILLUSTRATOR** Masha Laurence
**PRODUCTION DIRECTOR** Stephen Lang
**PRODUCTION CONTROLLER** Sumayyah Waheed

Colour reproduction by p2d

Printed in China by RR Donnelley Asia Printing Solution Limited

The authorised representative in the EEA is Penguin Random House Ireland, Morrison Chambers, 32 Nassau Street, Dublin D02 YH68.

Penguin Random House is committed to a sustainable future for our business, our readers and our planet. This book is made from Forest Stewardship Council® certified paper.